Maggie Lane's

NEEDLEPOINT
PILLOWS

BOOKS BY MAGGIE LANE

Needlepoint by Design
More Needlepoint by Design
Chinese Rugs Designed for Needlepoint
Rugs and Wall Hangings

Maggie Lane's
NEEDLEPOINT
PILLOWS

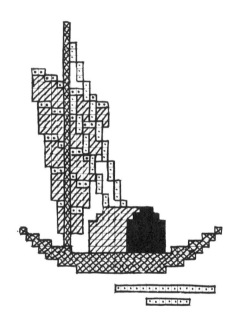

CHARLES SCRIBNER'S SONS
New York

Copyright © 1976, 1972, 1970 Maggie Lane
This book is a collection of designs from the author's first two
books, NEEDLEPOINT BY DESIGN and MORE NEEDLEPOINT BY DESIGN, and
one new pattern prepared for this edition.

Library of Congress Cataloging in Publication Data

Lane, Maggie.
    Maggie Lane's needlepoint pillows.

    1. Canvas embroidery—Patterns. 2. Pillows.
3. Design, Decorative—China. I. Title.
II. Title: Needlepoint pillows.
TT778.C3L32   746.9′7   76-24824
ISBN 0-684-14760-2
ISBN 0-684-14724-6 pbk.

This book published simultaneously in the
United States of America and in Canada—
Copyright under the Berne Convention

All rights reserved. No part of this book
may be reproduced in any form without the
permission of Charles Scribner's Sons.

1 3 5 7 9 11 13 15 17 19 MD/P 20 18 16 14 12 10 8 6 4 2
1 3 5 7 9 11 13 15 17 19 MD/C 20 18 16 14 12 10 8 6 4 2

Printed in the United States of America

Contents

Introduction

In many ways working needlepoint from a graph has been most rewarding for me. Once I have started a canvas I find it difficult to stop. Because I seldom color a graph I do not know what the finished design will look like when worked in the colors I have selected. So I push on until I have worked an area large enough so that the design begins to reveal the secret of its ultimate character. This is usually so tantalizing that I work far longer than I should. It has frequently been said to me that it must take the patience of Job to do the kind of work I do. My answer is always that it takes impatience. You see, it is hard to wait for the moment when the last stitch has been worked and I finally hold the finished pillow in my hands. The excitement I feel then is my reward and is worth the many hours of work and impatience.

Many of the persons to whom I have taught my method of doing needlepoint have told me that they too have worked long hours, even far into the night, because of an intense desire to see how the design will look after they have done "just this one bit more." The person working on a painted canvas derives no such thrill from the drama unfolding before the eyes. For them the design exists from the beginning and they need only to cover it with wool.

Each person I have taught has also described to me the pleasure felt when the complexities of the design were at last worked out on the canvas. Their sense of accomplishment was akin to that experienced after the solving of a difficult puzzle.

This book is written primarily for the beginner, who has never worked needlepoint on a painted canvas. It is also for the accomplished needleworker who is willing to try something more challenging than covering a painted pattern.

This is a teaching book. In it I shall show you, step by step, how to do needlework from a design worked out on graph paper. Symmetry and precision of detail are best achieved by this method and perfection is the result.

Turn to the back of the book where you will find a series of designs in graph form. You will also see illustrations showing many of these designs as finished works.

Although the book deals with pillows, the method and the designs can be used to make many other things. We shall consider them later (page 29).

Each design, like a small Chinese rug, has a central motif and a border. If you particularly like one border but prefer the central motif shown with a different border you are free to follow your own taste. All the central motifs in the square designs will combine well with any of the squared borders. You therefore have a wide variety of combinations from which to make a selection.

These central motifs and borders, originally having been conceived as small rugs, are uniquely suited for rugmaking. Instead of using #12 canvas you can use #10 mono or #8 penelope canvas. You can order it from Boutique Margot, 26 West 54th Street, New York City, 10019.

You can make 25″ square rugs or plan larger rugs, making your own graphs following the instructions given on page 22. When working on #8 canvas use 3 strands of Persian yarn.

When you finish your rug it is best to have it blocked, sized, bound, and lined by a professional.

When you have decided which border and which central motif you wish to use, two more basic decisions must be made before you can actually begin your needlework. Both decisions further affect the way the rugs or pillows will look because they determine the choice of yarns for your work.

Tonal Value

With few exceptions the patterns are designed to be worked in three tones, light, medium, and dark.

Black and white mark the outer limits in tonal value. There is nothing darker than black nor lighter than white. When the two are used together they generate more visual excitement than two shades of gray used together. Also, when a light pattern is used against a dark background it looks more dramatic than the reverse. So, if drama and excitement are what you want in your pillow, choose a dark tone for the background and a light tone for the pattern. If, however, you want a more subdued effect, choose a more medium tone for the background and a medium light, rather than white, for the pattern. The closer the tonal value the greater the loss of contrast, therefore the greater the loss of drama and excitement, and the more subtle the effect.

Color

When selecting the colors for your pillow I would suggest that you first consider the colors in the room, the most important one being that of the sofa or chair where you plan to place your finished pillow. I do hope you do not intend to put it on a sofa or chair upholstered in printed fabric. Design upon design is sometimes very effective, but I believe that these designs look best against plain fabrics.

I planned most of the designs for one basic color which is generally used for the background. The center motif and the border pattern are usually worked in white or off-white, with only one accent color for added interest. The pillows were planned this way because I believe in using restraint when it comes to the number of colors woven together in a small area. In an 18″ square the use of too many colors could result in chaos. I design with beauty and serenity in mind.

If your sofa or chair is medium blue, for example, the rug beige, the walls off-white, and the accent color grass-green, I offer the following schemes for your pillow:

1. Off-white and beige for the central motif and border.
    Grass-green for the accent color in central motif and in border.
    The blue of your sofa or chair as the background color.

2. Light blue, same color as sofa but lighter tone, for the central motif and border.
    Dark blue, perhaps toward navy, for accent color in central motif and border.
    The blue of your sofa or chair as the background color.
    This is known as a monochromatic combination, meaning that a single color is used, tonal contrast alone providing the interest.

3. Medium and dark blue for the central motif.
    Bitter grass-green for the accent color in central motif and border.
    Beige or off-white for background color.

4. Off-white and beige for central motif and border.
    Dark blue or navy for accent color.
    Bitter grass-green for background color.

Notes on Color

Color: "The quality in virtue of which objects present different appearances to the eye, in respect of the kind of light reflected from their surfaces." THE OXFORD UNIVERSAL DICTIONARY, 1955.

What a dry description of a quality that has aroused emotions from the beginning of time! Red, white and blue, for instance, call up the feeling of loyalty to the flag. Blue alone can make us think of the sea or the sky, or of Monday's moods. Yellow represents either the sun or cowardice. Green stands for verdure or envy, and red can mean either roses or anger, etc.

There are three primary and three secondary colors. Red, yellow and blue are the primaries. A primary color IS and cannot be achieved by a mixture of colors. The secondary colors, orange, green and violet, are the results of the mixture of two primary colors; red and yellow make orange, yellow and blue make green, and blue and red make violet. We see the total range of colors in the rainbow: red, orange, yellow, green, blue and violet.

When you place the colors on a color wheel they read as shown, each color opposite to its complement.

If you like you can slip the tertiary colors in the circle: red-orange goes between red and orange, orange-yellow between orange and yellow, yellow-green between yellow and green, etc.

Although you will not be mixing pigments to obtain the colors for your wools, the following information may prove helpful to you when you select the colors for your work.

When white is added to a color its tonal value is lightened. Its tonal value can be darkened

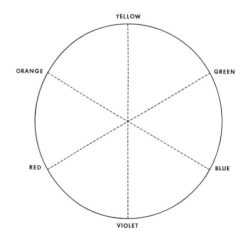

by the addition of a dark neutral, such as brown, gray or black. (However, the chromatic value of the color will be slightly reduced by the addition of the dark neutral. The very word "neutral" should tell you the added darkener will neutralize somewhat.) When you place two different colors next to each other you can easily see which color is the lighter of the two by half-closing your eyes, or squinting, while looking at them. NEVER use together, side by side, two different colors of the same tonal value UNLESS you want visual vibrations.

Going further we learn that a pure color, red, for instance, injected with a drop of its complement, green, will become slightly less intense. The more of the complement we add to the original color the more it loses its brilliance until it finally reaches the absolutely neutral state when in our case it is half red and half green, and is no longer either red or green.

So now we know that color has three qualities: 1) its hue, i.e., red or yellow or blue; 2) its tonal value, i.e., its lightness or darkness; 3) its chromatic value, i.e., its brilliance, intensity or neutrality.

Colors, like notes on the piano, make music. Some seem to melt together and harmonize while others clash in a disagreeable and atonal way. But *there are no ugly colors.* For every color you think of as unattractive there exists a color or combination of two colors which, when placed beside your "ugly" color, makes it beautiful.

Take, for example, eggplant; not a particularly handsome color when seen by itself, but frame it with putty and robin's egg blue and you have a beautiful chord. Or maroon with turquoise and cream. Or greenish fawn with teal blue. Some of the schemes I have used have come to my notice by accident. I have a camphor chest full of yarns and when I am ready to begin work on canvas I go to the coffer and pull out all the wool. Sometimes two or three skeins fall close together, the colors harmonizing so beautifully that I wonder why I never before thought of that combination. One such trio was a muted amethyst, cognac and a clay white.

When selecting your colors remember that the more muted the scheme, the more subtle must be the kind of white you use. The Persian yarns offer many shades of white from greenish through blue and neutral to a warm, rich cream.

Only when you plan to use black or a sharp, clear color for your main hue should you select pure white to use with it.

In *The Tiffany Studio Collection of Antique Chinese Rugs*, printed at Hillacre, Riverside, Connecticut, for the Tiffany Studios, 1908, there appears a short chapter on the colors that were employed by the Chinese rug weavers. The first paragraph points to the basic difference between Chinese rugs and those made in other parts of the eastern world. The observation is made that primary red never appears in Chinese rugs. Instead, the weavers used fruit colors such as apricot, persimmon, pomegranate and peach, all these colors being warmed with gold. In Persian rugs, on the other hand, reds of great brilliance and depth were used, many of them verging on cerise or magenta, both violet-reds. It is then pointed out that the Chinese limited themselves to a narrow palette, two or three colors, but four or five tones, i.e.: "two shades of yellow, two shades of blue, and one of cream"; or "two shades of blue, cream and apricot red." Other eastern rugmakers used a wide range of colors and tones, i.e.: "yellow, two shades of blue, cream, several shades of green, fire-color, turquoise-blue and many shades of red."

Here I would like to make an observation of my own on two additional qualities that make Chinese rugs unique:

1. Patterned areas are usually relieved by plain fields.

2. There is always a serene well-scaled border, echoing the colors and tones used in the patterns in the field.

When a designer limits his range of color to two or three, he must offer something else to create interest in his design. Pattern is the answer, and pattern is created only by differences in tonal value.

I have noted here for you the characteristics of antique Chinese rugs because they set standards of excellence that were my guide and goal when I created the designs in this book.

Materials

Before you can proceed further you will need the following materials and tools:

Canvas

In most needlework stores two types of needlepoint canvas are available. They are *penelope* canvas and *mono* canvas.

Penelope Canvas is a double-thread canvas. The intersections of the double threads are woven together. This locks the intersections. The canvas is therefore good for the half-cross stitch. But since we shall not be working the half-cross stitch we shall not be using penelope canvas.

Mono Canvas is a single-thread canvas that looks like screening except that it is woven with cotton threads rather than with wire. It comes in white and also in an unbleached or ecru form. (I prefer the latter because it keeps its crispness longer.) *Mono canvas is best suited to our needs* because the holes in the canvas, i.e., the spaces between the warp and woof threads, are larger than those on penelope canvas. So working on mono canvas is less tiring to the eyes than working on penelope canvas.

Mono canvas comes in several mesh counts, i.e., the

mesh, or the intersections of the evenly spaced warp and woof threads, range from 10 to the running inch up to 40 to the inch. This latter count is actually a fine gauze and we need not consider it. Canvas with 12 threads to the inch, which I shall call #12 canvas, is the mesh for which I designed, and on which I made my pillows.

When you work, each stitch will cover one intersection of the warp and woof threads of the canvas. So on #12 canvas you will work 12 stitches to the running inch, or 144 stitches to the square inch.

NOTE: If you want to make your pillow larger or smaller than the size indicated on the graph use a different count of canvas. For a larger pillow use #10 canvas and for a smaller one use #14 or even #16 canvas, depending on how small you want your pillow to be. The way to estimate the size of the finished pillow follows: if the graph measures 201 small box-stitches in width and 201 small box-stitches in height, divide 201 by the number of threads to the inch on the canvas you intend to use. #10 canvas will make a pillow about 20″ square, #12 canvas will make a pillow about 17″ square, #14 a pillow about 14½″ square, and # 16 about 13″ square. There is always a small difference between the exact size you figure your pillow will measure and the size of the outline you will draw after counting off the canvas threads. This is due to slight irregularities in the spacing of the canvas threads.

Good canvas is made of firm fibers of even thickness. It is sized to keep it crisp and fresh while you work on it. The sizing also keeps the intersections of the threads in place. The more highly polished the threads the better the canvas. The unbleached canvas of which I spoke earlier has threads more highly polished than those of bleached, white mono canvas.

When you select canvas, look for a piece that has no flaws, like knots or uneven threads in it. You want no weakness in the material on which you are going to spend your precious time and effort.

Buy a piece of canvas large enough to allow for a 3″ margin on all sides around the area you plan to cover with needlework. Since most of the designs were created for pillows which would measure 17″–18″ square when worked on #12 canvas you will need the following sizes of canvas depending on the count of canvas you select:

> 26″ square for #10 canvas
> 24″ square for #12 canvas
> 21″ square for #14 canvas
> 19″ square for #16 canvas

Binding the Raw Edges of Your Canvas. Use masking tape 1″ wide, or fabric binding sewn on by hand or machine. I use the masking tape. It serves the purpose for which it was intended, namely, to keep the edges of the canvas from raveling as you work. It is quickly and easily applied. I am usually so anxious to get to the actual needlework that I bless all short cuts that serve me well.

Needles

Buy Boye tapestry needles, #18 for #12 canvas.

Thimble

Use one. I live in mine.

Scissors

Use a pair of small, sharp-pointed ones.

Wools

There are several types of wool you can use for needle-point. Knitting and crocheting wools are not among them. They will not do because they have short, fluffy fibers and therefore are not strong. Needlepoint wools must have the strength of long fibers, for you will be pulling each thread many times through the canvas. Select your wools from the following types:

Crewel Wool is a springy two-ply yarn that can be used on #12 canvas, two threads covering it very well.

Persian Wool comes in a very wide range of colors and has a 3-strand thread which is readily separated into single strands. Use 2 strands to cover #12 canvas.

Tapestry Wool is a well-twisted yarn that covers #12 canvas perfectly just as it comes from the hank.

Other Yarns

Silk. The floss comes from France. It is more expensive than wool. It comes in 9-yard skeins. If you want to use it for a change of texture, use all the 7 threads that cling together as you take them from the skein. You may experience some difficulty in working with silk. It is hard to run the needle through the back of your silk when you want to anchor a new thread, and frequently one of the single threads among the several with which you are working will turn stubborn and make a loop on the surface of your work. Then you will have to stop and pull your thumbnail along the threads as yet unworked. This often snags and pulls the loop out of the worked stitch.

Cotton. Use D.M.C. cotton which comes in a good range of colors, each well shaded from light to dark. Use the group of threads that adhere together, thread them through the needle, and use them double for #12 canvas. (You may have the same trouble with cotton as you have with silk. See above for solution.)

Silver and Gold Thread. This beautiful thread comes from France. D.M.C. is the brand to buy. Experiment to see how many threads you need to use to cover your canvas. Silver and gold threads can also be used with strands of D.M.C. cotton floss to produce a duller effect, like cloth of silver or gold. Use pale gray with the silver, and soft maize or buff with the gold.

Frames

You will NOT need a frame for your work. The stitches you will be using are all stitches that require a single thrust of the needle into and out of the canvas. If you were to stretch your canvas on a frame it would become taut. You would then have to use two motions for each stitch. One hand would have to be in front of the canvas to insert the needle, the other hand behind the canvas to return the needle to the front of the canvas again, a slower process than the single in and out thrust mentioned above.

Stitches

Flat Stitches

NOTE: All flat stitches should be worked to slant in the same direction, i.e., each stitch should look like a grain of rice tilted from upper right to lower left.

Continental Stitch. For single-row outlining ONLY. If this stitch is used as background stitch, it distorts the canvas severely.

CONTINENTAL STITCH

Basket-Weave Stitch. This stitch is for background work and all filling wherever there is more than a single line of stitching needed. The basket-weave pulls the canvas askew less than any other simple background stitch. In addition you can work your stitches without having to turn your canvas around all the time. For these reasons I recommend it.

Special Note About Working the Basket-Weave: Never work two rows of basket-weave in the same direction. If you do, a diagonal line will show faintly on the surface of your work. Also, when casting off the ends of your threads and running in the new threads you want to anchor preparatory to working, do it in random directions. If you follow a directional pattern cast-

The basket-weave or the tent stitch, showing the right and the wrong way to work if you want to work with the weave of the canvas. The left diagram shows the right way; the right shows the wrong way: against the weave.

BASKET-WEAVE (right)   BASKET-WEAVE (wrong)

 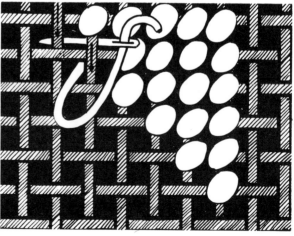

ing off and running in, it will also show faintly as a directional pattern on the surface of your work.

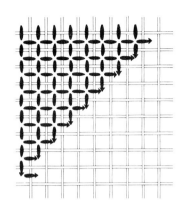

You can tell where you should begin your next row by looking at the back of your work. If the threads of the just completed row run horizontally on the back of your canvas (see illustration) you must start at the upper left-hand side on the front of the canvas. If the threads of the just completed row run vertically on the back of your canvas (see illustration) you must start at the lower right-hand side on the front of the canvas.

Working with the Weave of the Canvas: During the years I worked only on mono canvas I made a startling discovery. When doing the basket-weave, all stitches should be keyed to the weave of the canvas.

My discovery occurred one day when I was working with black wool on white canvas. After a time I hung my work over a chair back at a distance from me so I could view my design objectively. It was then I noticed that my background stitches, up to a clearly visible diagonal line, covered the white canvas completely, and beyond that line they allowed the white canvas to peek through here and there with annoying frequency. I turned the canvas over and looked at the back of it. I found that two rows, worked in the same direction, corresponded to the line on the surface separating the stitches that covered the canvas from those that permitted a bit of canvas to show. I then examined the relationship of my stitches to the weave of the canvas.

As you know, needlepoint canvas is a loosely woven mesh made up of horizontal and vertical threads. These threads weave over and under each other to form the intersections which our stitches will cover. Each vertical thread weaves over and under horizontal threads. Each horizontal thread weaves over and under vertical threads. I call it a bridge when one thread humps over another. Horizontal bridges appear in diagonal rows. Vertical bridges appear in diagonal rows. A row of horizontal bridges is followed by a row of vertical bridges, which in turn is followed by a row of horizontal bridges, and so on. When working your diagonal rows of basket-weave stitches, you should work the uphill rows to cover the diagonal rows of *horizontal* canvas thread bridges, and your downhill rows to cover the diagonal rows of *vertical* canvas thread bridges.

Once you have learned to key your stitches to the weave of the canvas, you will find that you need never worry about where to begin the next row of needlepoint. You will also discover that no matter where you choose to work on your canvas, all rows of needlepoint will mesh properly when they meet each other.

The Brick Stitch. This stitch needs fat thread. Work it up and down to produce a texture that looks like laid bricks. The first row is numbered. The second row is lettered. The back of the stitch looks like a basket-weave.

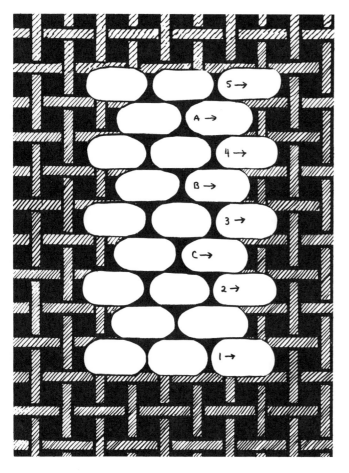

BRICK STITCH

The Eyelet Stitch combines with a filler of continental stitches in the Serenity Pillow II.

The Jacquard Stitch. This works up into a handsome diagonal zigzag. It pulls the canvas out of shape somewhat so try not to pull your thread hard when you work this stitch.

The Irish Stitch is used in the outer border of the Geometric pillow.

JACQUARD STITCH

IRISH STITCH

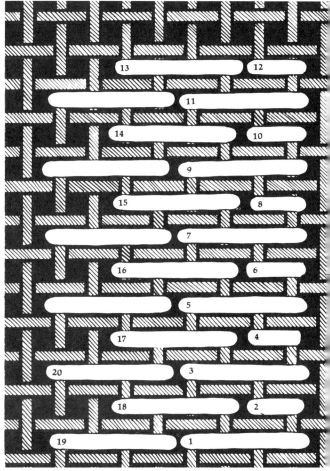

Bump Stitches

The Smyrna Cross Stitch. The diagram shows the four steps in making the stitch; the two threads in the first, the x-shaped cross, and the two threads in the second, the +-shaped cross.

SMYRNA CROSS STITCH   **DOUBLE LEVIATHAN STITCH**

The Double Leviathan Stitch. Make a large X stitch, then an oblique X over one arm of step one, then over the other arm of step one. Finally make an upright cross stitch over the whole preceding six strands. IF YOU END THE STITCH WITH A VERTICAL THREAD, AS SHOWN, END ALL SUCCEEDING STITCHES WITH A VERTICAL THREAD. IF YOU END THE STITCH WITH A HORIZONTAL THREAD, END ALL SUCCEEDING STITCHES WITH A HORIZONTAL THREAD.

The Double Straight Cross Stitch. Make sure that all final threads cross the stitches in the same direction.

DOUBLE STRAIGHT CROSS STITCH

TRIPLE CROSS STITCH

Triple Cross Stitch. This is a bump stitch worked over three horizontal and three vertical threads. It is for use in the center of patterns which have an uneven number of stitches in their width and length, thus having a center axis.

Double Straight Cross Stitches are arranged to form a diamond.

NOTE: All bump stitches should be finished with the final thread running from top to bottom, with the exception of the triple cross. Its final thread has to run from upper right of center to lower left of center.

Starting to Work

You now have in front of you the following: a piece of bound canvas, wool, needles, a thimble, and a pair of scissors. You know the kind of design you are going to make, what colors you will use in the work, and you know how large your pillow will be when it is finished. You know how to make six basic flat stitches and four raised bump stitches. You wonder, now, how you are going to transfer the design from the graph to the canvas. The answer is that you will do it by reading from the graph as you work. This is like reading notes of music on a page and playing the notes with your fingers on an instrument. Here I quote from the book *Oriental Rugs in Colour* by Preben Liebetrau, page 17. He is talking about rugs made in the East. "Here the weaving is directed by a *salim*, as he is called, who recites or monotonously intones the design being copied. Or again, the design may first be set down in colour on squared paper, each square indicating a knot. The weaver follows this coloured chart much as the pianist follows his sheet-music.

"Beautiful results are obtained only through exact and careful workmanship."

Marking the Canvas

Fold the canvas in half, then in half again. In this way you will find the center of your canvas.

Mark the Horizontal and Vertical Centers of Your Canvas. Use an A. D. nylon-tipped marking pen, pale blue or light tan in color. Draw a dotted line ALONG the horizontal and vertical threads radiating from the center of your canvas. Do this only if there is an UNEVEN number of box-stitches on the graph you plan to follow. (SEE ILLUSTRATION BELOW.) Where there is an EVEN number of box-stitches on the graph draw the dotted lines for the horizontal and vertical centers BETWEEN two canvas threads.

Outline the Area to Be Worked. On the graph, count off the number of box-stitches from the center lines out to the

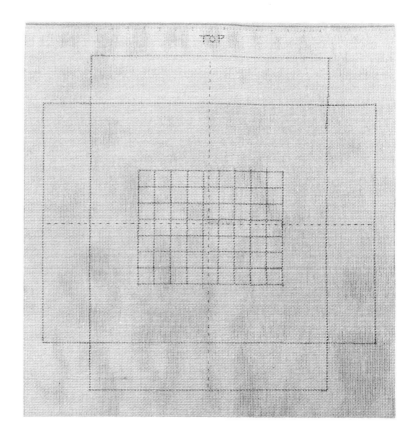

corners. If the whole graph measures 201 x 201 box-stitches, count off 100 canvas threads to the right and to the left of the vertical center of your canvas. Count off 100 canvas threads above and below the horizontal center of your canvas. Then draw the outlines around the area just counted. The outlines should enclose an area containing 201 threads across and 201 threads from top to bottom. NOTE: when drawing the outline do not draw the line ALONG a thread but BETWEEN the 100th thread and the 101st.

Mark Graph Lines on Canvas. An X marks the center box-stitch on your graph. This is where there is an uneven number of stitches to the graph. An X also marks the center of your canvas where the two center lines intersect. (⊞ marks the center of each graph with an even number of box-stitches.)

Each graph is made up of a cross-hatch of fine lines. These outline small squares, each of which represents a stitch. I have been calling them, and will continue to call them, BOX-STITCHES.

Every tenth line on the graph is a heavier, darker line. These lines outline squares containing 100 box-stitches. Duplicate these heavy lines on your canvas. The purpose of drawing these lines on the canvas is to create a frame of reference that corresponds to the grid of heavy lines on the graph. This will reduce the possibility of error in counting your stitches. (The squares you outline on your canvas will be filled with 100 stitches.)

IMPORTANT: Each box-stitch on the graph represents a crossing of a horizontal and a vertical canvas thread, or the stitch which will cover it, *not the hole between threads.* Conversely, each crossing of threads on the canvas corresponds to a box-stitch on the graph.

Mark the Top of Your Canvas with the Word "Top."

Mark the First Graph Line. Use a pale A. D. nylon-tipped marking pen. Never use a regular lead pencil on canvas. It always grays the wool. If on your graph three box-stitches separate the first heavy line ABOVE the center from the center box-stitch (with an X in it) count off three canvas threads ABOVE the horizontal center thread, then draw a horizontal line BETWEEN that third thread and the fourth. Similarly, if four box-stitches on your graph separate the first heavy line to the RIGHT from the center box-stitch (with the X) count off four canvas threads to the RIGHT of the vertical center thread, then draw a vertical line BETWEEN that fourth thread and the fifth. (SEE ILLUSTRATION PAGE 22.)

Now draw horizontal lines to separate rows of 10 horizontal threads, and vertical lines to separate rows of 10 vertical threads. Use the first 2 grid lines you drew as the lines from which you count off your rows of 10.

When you have finished you will have a canvas covered with a grid of faint lines corresponding to those on the graph. This will make it easy to do *Needlepoint by the Numbers.*

Let us finally begin needlework.

Working & Finishing

Specific instructions for each central motif and border start on page 31.

When I work I sit on a sofa with a light to my left. I place my graph to my right and use my small sewing scissors as a pointer to indicate, on the graph, the area from which I am reading at the moment. I do so from the beginning to the end of the "fancy work." After I have finished all the difficult pattern work I put away the graph. Then I can relax and enjoy filling in the background.

So thread your needle with the color you need to start your central motif. Place your scissors on the graph, points toward the first box-stitch you will make. Let us say this stitch is in the first square below the square containing the center box-stitch (with the X in it). Find the corresponding square on the canvas. Let us say that the first box-stitch, on the graph, is the third from the right side of the square, and the fourth up from the bottom side. On your canvas find the corresponding crossing of threads, and you are ready to make your first stitch.

Run your needle in basting stitches across 3"–4" of canvas until the point is next to the spot where you will make the first stitch. Make it, and you are on your way.

Follow the direction of box-stitches shown on the graph as you make your next stitches, and also count the number as you work. The heavy lines on the graph and the corresponding lines drawn on your canvas will help you in this respect, i.e., counting. Continue working until you have finished your first length of yarn. Then run the needle and yarn through 8–10 stitches on the underside of your work. Disengage the tail of the yarn you left at the beginning of work and thread it through the eye of the needle. Run it also through 8–10 stitches on the underside of your work. *Always clip off excess yarn* each time you finish a thread. Otherwise you will catch the ends of loose threads hanging from the back of your canvas. These threads may come through to the front of your work, and if they do they will prove very disturbing and annoying.

Re-thread your needle, run it through 8–10 stitches at the back of your work to anchor the tail end, then continue with your work.

When working develop an even rhythm. Never pull the thread hard. Instead, put the needle into and out of the canvas and then pull it, in a single motion, only until the yarn lies flat in the stitch. Roll the needle slightly, your thumb moving against your forefinger, *away* from the tip of the forefinger, toward the first knuckle joint. This will help to keep the thread from twisting.

Blocking the Canvas

Do Not Wet the Canvas. It is not necessary if you have used the basket-weave stitch. And wetting the canvas might cause the running of any ink lines drawn on it. Instead, block with a steam iron and damp or wet cloth. Place the cloth over the canvas and, while ironing, pull the canvas *hard* against the direction in which it has warped. Don't be afraid of it, it won't tear. Then pull from the sides, then from the top and bottom while the canvas is still hot and steamy. Correct the corners and press dry.

Finishing Touches

After I have steamed and blocked the canvas and before I cut off the excess canvas, to leave 8–10 threads outside the worked area, I use a sewing machine, set at 12 stitches to the inch, and stitch a zigzag or wavy row or two of stitching between the finished needlework and the seventh or eighth thread *away* from the finished needlework. Then when I cut the canvas it won't ravel.

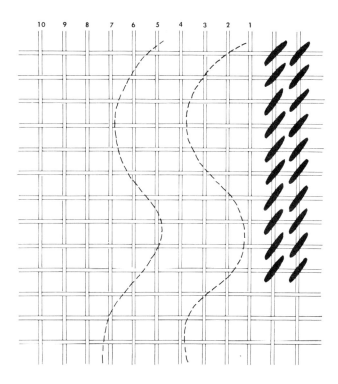

Sewing Fabric Back to Needlework

With the insides out, sew heavy silk fabric, matched as closely as possible to the background color, to the needlework. I pin the two together first, then sew with the machine. I sew the pieces together with the needlepoint piece on top so I can run my seam *between* the finished work and the next, uncovered canvas thread. Sew three sides of the square, and an inch or two on each side of the fourth side. Remove pins. Fold back the *fabric* flap on the unsewn side of the casing, press it so it will have a straight crease in it. Turn the casing right side out. From inside the casing push the corners out. Fill the casing with a custom-made pillow, 60-40 down and feathers. Pin the backing to the needlework on the unsewn side and slip-stitch the two together.

Although the pillows have been designed so they do not need a braid or welting, you may wish to add this finishing touch. I suggest you make a braid out of the same kind of yarn you used in the needlepoint.

Buy an uncut hank of the color of yarn you want. Unwind three lengths of wool about 6 or 7 yards long. Use a #7 Bates crochet hook and the three strands. Crochet a single chain-stitch braid long enough to edge the pillow. Sew the braid on the pillow after the casing has been filled with the down pillow.

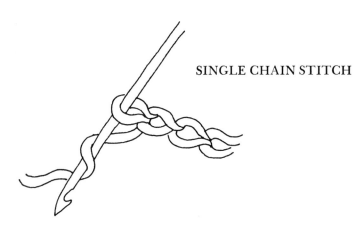

SINGLE CHAIN STITCH

Before pinning the braid to the casing to cover the scam joining the needlework to the fabric backing, tuck in the loose threads at each end of the braid threading them singly in your needlepoint needle and working them back into the braid. Then pin the braid to the pillow seam. NOTE: The flat side, that which looks like a braid, is the underside. Slip-stitch the braid to the pillow cover along the back, then along the front of the braid, i.e., two times around the pillow.

Although the central motifs were designed with pillows in mind they can be adapted to many other uses. One can make two squares—with the frog on one, the turtle on the other—and sew them together to create a very handsome tote bag, with, of course, added handles. Or a circular floral motif on the top of a needlepoint cover for a typewriter. Piano benches, foot stools, and chair seats can all be handsomely dressed in needlepoint using these designs. If the project requires some figuring on your part you can make your own graph. Buy one large sheet of 17″ x 22″ graph paper, or as many sheets as you will need, of the kind that has 100 box-stitches to the square inch. It is easy to count, and easy to read. It is the kind I use for designing.

If you want to make a piece of needlepoint 15″ square on #12 canvas, multiply 15 x 12. You will then outline a square on your graph 180 x 180 box-stitches. Work out your design within this area.

If you want to design your own central motif, outline the area that you wish it to fill on your graph. Rough it out on a separate sheet of paper, perfect the drawing, then trace it onto the graph paper. After this you must adapt it to the box-stitch lines of the graph paper, making the step-lines with which you are by now familiar, having seen them in all the graphs in this book.

You may color your graph if you like but do it lightly, otherwise you will obliterate the grid lines, making the graph difficult to read.

When your graph is finished proceed as directed in the instructions for making pillows.

If the area to be covered is irregular, such as that of a chair seat, take a piece of brown paper and make a pattern of the area. Cut off the excess, and outline the pattern on the canvas. Then find the center of the area on the canvas, mark off horizontal and vertical lines and the graph lines, and proceed as directed in the pillow instructions.

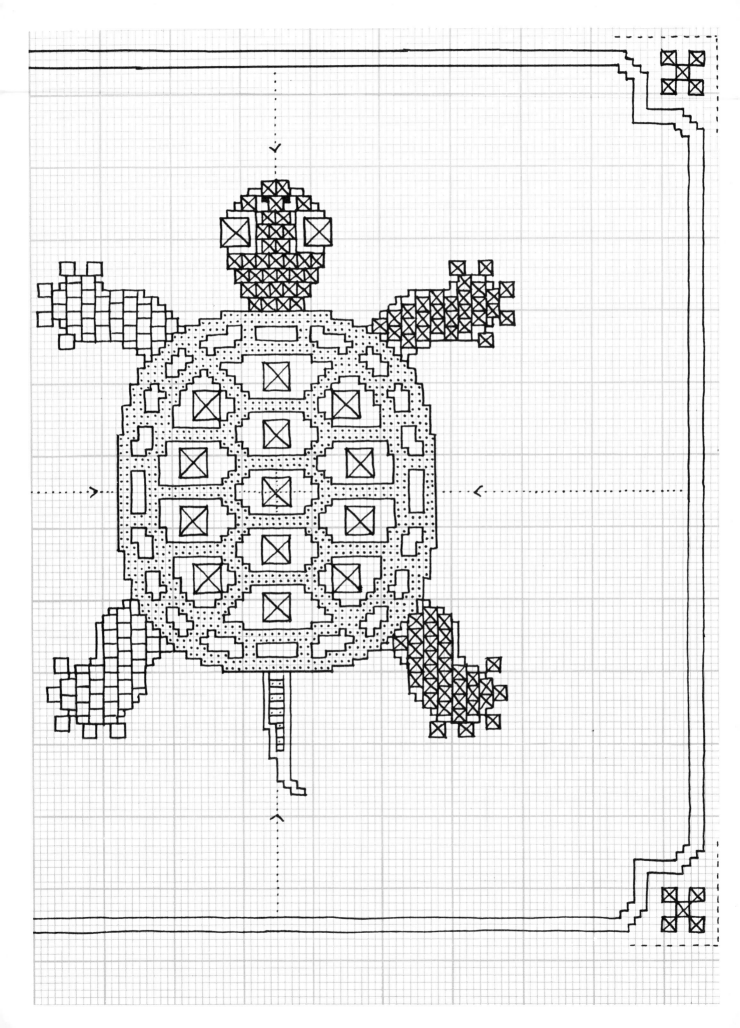

Turtle Pillow

17" x 17"

The turtle pillow measures 202 threads by 202 threads. Bind a piece of #12 canvas measuring 21" x 21". Mark two center lines, then outline pillow and draw graph lines in the area where you will work the turtle.

The following 4 tones and colors are suggested for the turtle pillow:

1. Light   White
2. Medium light   Light Beige
3. Medium tone   Amber
4. Medium dark or dark   Olive Green or Black

Dotted lines intersect in the middle of the double Leviathan stitch square in the center of the turtle's back. Where they cross marks the center of the graph and corresponds to the place on your canvas where the two center lines meet. Use this point for reference when you begin work.

1. Using #2 tone work outer outline of turtle's shell. Work inner outline of turtle's shell. Work separations between thirteen lozenges on turtle's shell. Work separations between inner and outer outlines of shell.

2. Using #1 tone work double Leviathan lumps in each of the thirteen lozenges. Fill in remainder of each lozenge and also white areas in frame of shell. Work outline of tail and white lines in tail, then using #2 tone, work dotted or shaded lines in tail.

3. Using #1 tone work head, up to eye level, in Smyrna cross stitch. The stitches not crossed in head, arms, and legs will be worked as regular, flat stitches. Using #2 tone work the outline around eyes. Using #3 tone work double Leviathan lumps for eyes. Finish head up to nostrils, working again in #1 tone. Using #4 tone work two nostrils, then finish head. Using #1 tone work Smyrna cross stitches in arms and legs, and fill in flat stitches in same tone. Work 5 Smyrna cross stitches for fingernails and toenails on each appendage.

4. Using #2 tone work two-row outline around field, i.e., the one with the in-turning corners.

5. Using #2 tone work 5 lumps in each corner, outside outline worked in step 4.

6. Using #1 tone work key fret border.

7. Using #4 tone work background within field border, then background to key fret border.

8. Using #2 tone work 6-line outer border.

Frog Pillow

17½" x 17½"

The frog pillow measures 207 threads by 207 threads. Bind a piece of #12 canvas measuring 22" square. Mark the outlines, the center threads, and the graph lines where you will work the frog.

The following tones are suggested for the frog:

1. Pure white
2. Off-white
3. Light neutral
4. Medium tone. Accent color
5. Medium dark tone. Background color
6. Dark tone, like navy or black

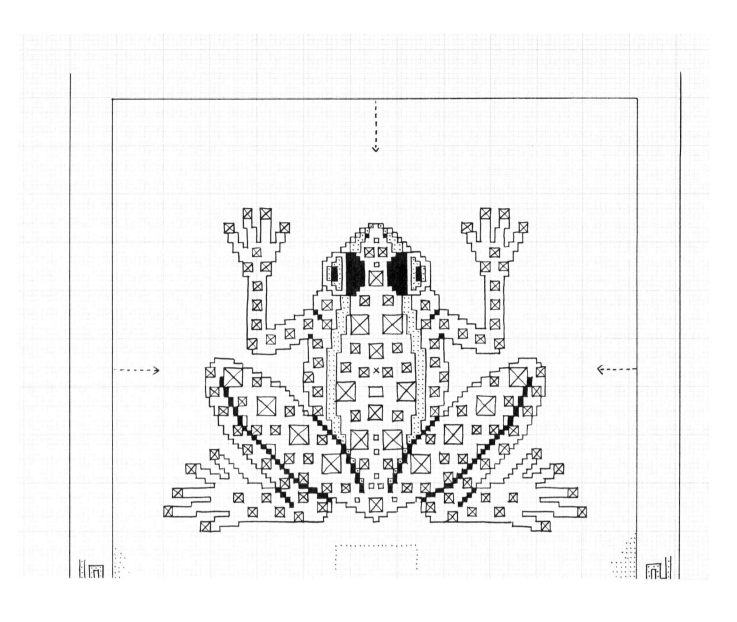

NOTE: On the graph an X in the center of the frog's back represents the intersection of the center threads of the canvas. Use it for reference when you begin work.

1. Using #3 tone work eyelids and outline lines within body, those at shoulders, and outlining legs. They are marked in black on the graph.

2. Using #1 tone work stripes on frog's body. They are dotted or shaded on the graph and run from the lower part of the frog's body up to the tip of his nose.

3. Using #4 tone, the accent color, work lumps on frog.

4. Using #1 tone work white outline around iris and pupil area of eyes. Use #4 tone, accent color, for iris and #6 tone for black pupil in each eye. Work #6 tone nostril.

5. Using #2 tone outline frog's body, then fill in.

6. Using #1 tone work Smyrna cross stitches for finger- and toenails.

7. Using #5 tone, background color, work key fret.

8. Using #2 tone work background of key fret.

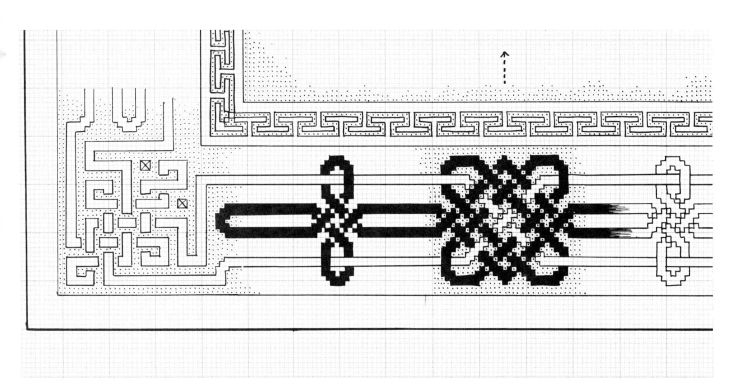

9. Using #5 tone fill in background within border.

10. Using #2 tone work corner motifs and broken x bands in outer border.

11. Using #4 tone work 2 lumps in each corner motif.

12. Using #4 tone work "frog" knots and bows in border. They are marked in black on the graph.

13. Using #5 tone work background of outer border.

14. Using #2 tone work 7-row band at outer edge of pillow.

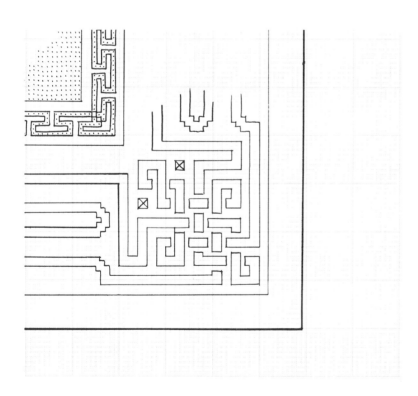

TOP

Serenity Pillow I
16" x 16"

The pillow measures 192 threads by 192 threads. Bind a piece of #12 canvas measuring 20" x 20". Mark the center lines and the outlines. Then mark the graph lines in the center where you will work the octagon motif. (The central design is a combination of the 8 trigrams from the "I Ching," and a stylized version of a Chinese character for happiness.)

Three tones are used in the Serenity pillow:

1. Light
2. Medium
3. Dark

Suggested colors in Persian wool:

1. 017 gray-white
2. 145 tobacco brown
3. 117 eggplant

Many handsome combinations of colors are possible here: White, gray, and black: gray-white, cognac, and eggplant: White, bitter green, and navy: white, saffron yellow, and burnt-orange, etc.

⁜ marks the center of the graph and corresponds to the crossing of the center lines on the canvas.

1. Using #1 tone work the character in the center of the octagon motif. Work the outline around it. This line circles the shaded, or dotted, area, the background for the character. Work the outline of the octagon, then the eight trigrams.

2. Using #3 tone fill in shaded area around central character.

3. Using #2 tone fill in background behind eight trigrams (the background in the octagonal collar around the central character).

4. Using #1 tone work outline around field. This is the band, two stitches wide, with in-turning corners. (See next page.)

5. Using #2 tone work Smyrna cross stitches in the field, within the area just outlined.

6. With #1 tone work inner and outer bands outlining swastika border.

7. With #3 tone work Smyrna cross stitches in area between band worked in step 4 and the inner band of the swastika border. These stitches are represented, on the graph, by shaded, or dotted, squares. And at each corner there is a large square, a double Leviathan stitch, surrounded by four Smyrna cross stitches.

8. Using #3 tone fill in field.

9. Using #2 tone fill in area directly outside the in-turning outline of the field. In step 7 you worked the bumps in this band.

10. Using #1 tone work swas-
    tikas.

11. Using #3 tone work back-
    ground of swastika border,
    dotted, or shaded, on the
    graph.

12. Using #2 tone work outer
    border of pillow, the band 7
    stitches deep.

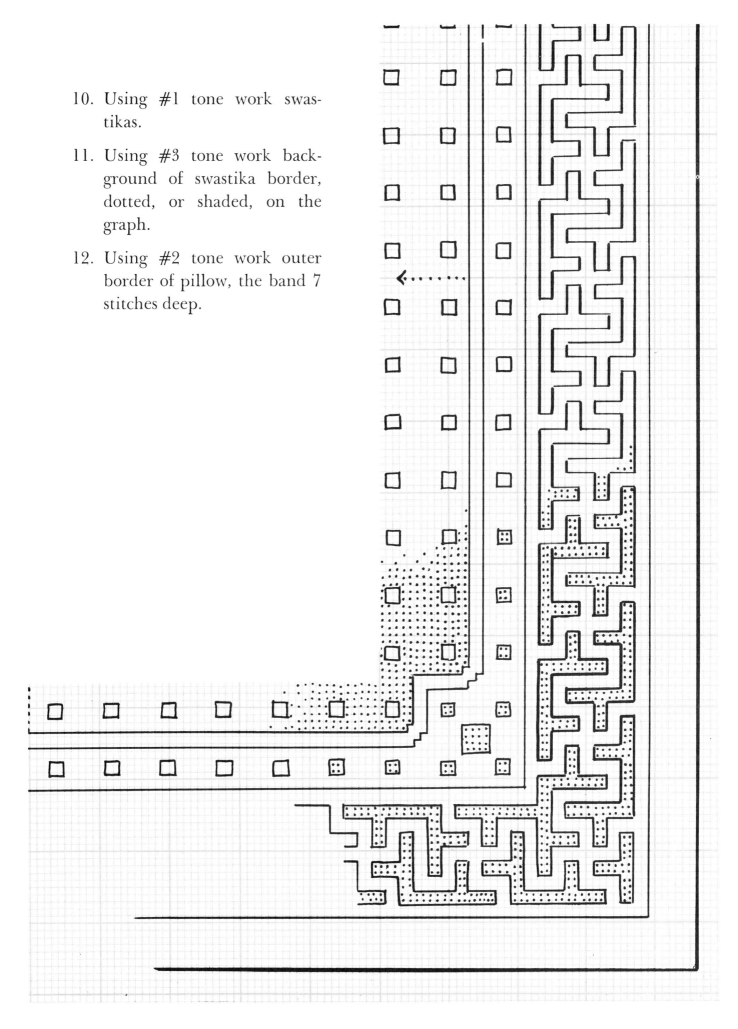

Serenity Pillow II
17" x 17"

The pillow measures 200 threads by 200 threads. Bind a piece of #12 canvas measuring 21" x 21". Mark vertical and horizontal center lines. Outline the pillow. Draw graph lines within the work area.

There are three tones in the design:

1. Light
2. Medium
3. Dark

1. Using #1 tone work central character and circle around it.

2. Using #2 tone fill in background around central character.

3. Using #3 tone work single inner row of bands outlining field.

4. Using #1 tone work white outer borders of bow-shaped corner pieces.

5. Using #3 tone work shaded inner borders of bow-shaped corner pieces.

6. Using #2 tone work eyelet stitch in field. See page 17.

7. Using #3 tone fill in background around eyelets.

8. Using #2 tone work Smyrna cross stitches in bow-shaped corner pieces. Then fill in with #2 tone.

9. Using #3 tone work outlines of the band between the outer swastika border and the line outlining field. Smyrna cross stitches dot the band you are now outlining. These are also to be worked in #3 tone.

10. Using #2 tone fill in background of band you have just outlined and dotted in step 9.

11. Using #3 tone work swastikas.

12. Using #1 tone fill in remainder of pillow, i.e., between dotted band and outline of field, and behind swastikas out to the edge of the pillow.

13. Block and finish pillow.

Island Temple Scenic Pillow
12" x 15½" x 2½" boxing

The pillow measures 141 threads by 187 threads. Bind a piece of #12 canvas 16" x 20". Mark center threads, mark four outlines, then draw graph lines in the work area.

Six tones are used in the Island Temple Scenic. They are:

1. White
2. Light
3. Light medium
4. Medium
5. Medium dark
6. Dark

A scenic design worked in five shades of blue and an off-white

Island Temple
Scenic Pillow
I

PANEL B

The original pillow was made with Persian wool. The key to the colors used follows:

1. 017 off-white
2. 386 light blue
3. 385 light medium blue
4. 330 medium blue
5. 334 medium dark blue
6. 365 navy blue

This design was adapted from the decoration on an antique Oriental Lowestoft porcelain mug in my possession. The piece is in blue and white with the delightful texture of an "orange-peel" glaze. It sits on my desk and holds my pens and pencils. One day I picked it up and, for the first time, looked at it intently. The wealth of detail it revealed excited me, and I then sat down to graph its design for needlepoint.

When I had finished the scene for the face of the pillow, I felt that it needed needlepoint boxing. So I searched through my Oriental lacquer books until I found the appropriate design, a case with rounded corners and floral panels. I adapted these to suit my pillow pattern and I began my needlework.

I was so pleased by the resulting pillow that I made a mirror image of it, with one small change: a sailboat takes the

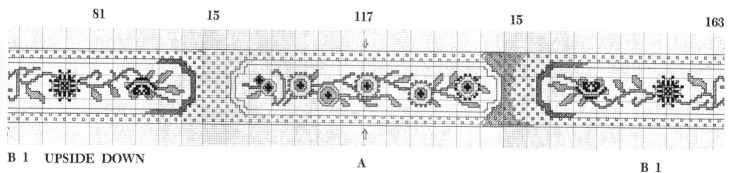

B 1   UPSIDE DOWN   A   B 1

place of one of the small islands of rocks in the original. At a later date I even augmented the design further, giving it a border so I could use it as a graph for an area rug worked on #7 penelope canvas.

Since the original design was taken from a porcelain piece I like to think of it in antique glaze-like colors, worked in tones of blues, or greens, or lavenders, or perhaps even ranging from deep coral to faint bittersweet.

I have prepared the graph with tonal symbols in each box-stitch so no instructions are necessary for the placement of tones.

The Boxing Band

The work area in the band measures about 53″ in length and 2½″ in width. Bind a piece of #12 canvas 58″ in length and 6″ in width. Count off an area 620 threads in length by 31 threads in width. The floral panels will be placed on it as shown below.

After outlining the panel areas, mark the graph lines in each one. Again, the graph has been drawn with tonal symbols in the squares so no instructions are necessary for the placement of tones.

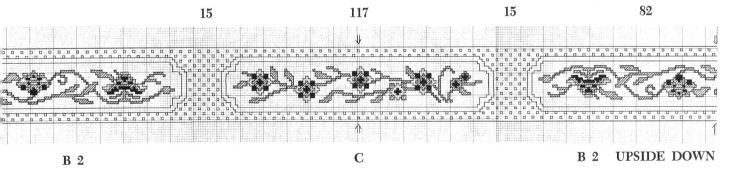

15   117   15   82

B 2   C   B 2   UPSIDE DOWN

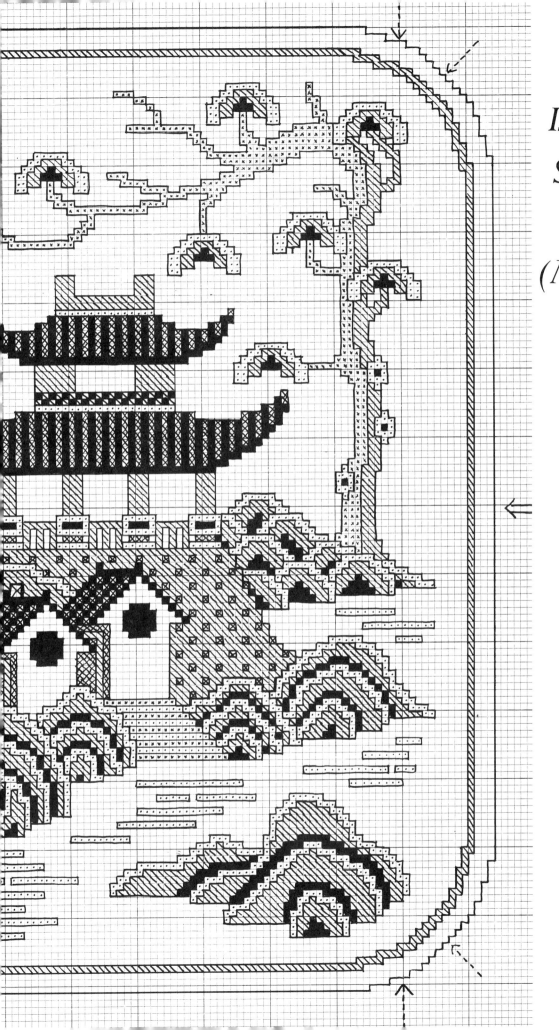

Island Temple

Scenic Pillow

II

(Mirror Image)

Putting the Pillow Together

Before you sew the boxing to the face of the pillow, take a piece of brown wrapping paper and draw on it the exact shape and size of the pillow's worked area. (Here I refer only to the face of the pillow.) Cut the paper to this size. Use it when you prepare the backing for the pillow. Place the paper pattern on the heavy, off-white silk and wool fabric you have chosen to match the off-white in the pillow's background. Use a pale gray coloring pencil and, on the fabric, draw a line around the paper pattern. Then, using the sewing machine, sew a line of off-white basting stitches along this gray line. With the same pencil, lightly mark the center lines on the top, the bottom, the two sides, and the four rounded corners of the backing. Allowing a ⅝" seam allowance, cut around the row of basting stitches.

Now, sew the two ends of the banding together. Do it by hand, using #4 tone wool. Be sure to match the pattern at one end to the pattern at the other end of the banding. Press seam open. (The seam allowances on this seam will NOT be caught in the seam that joins the banding to the face of the pillow.)

Placing seam at bottom center, pin side of banding to face of pillow. Matching center lines at top, at sides, at four corners, and of course at bottom, sew seam by hand using #1 tone wool. (Do not catch in seam allowance of banding while sewing the around-the-pillow seam.) Press seam toward boxing. Turn right side out.

Place custom-made pillow in pillow case. Turn under raw edge of boxing band. It will meet the basting line on the backing. Put backing in place on back of pillow and pin boxing band to basted seam line, matching the eight center marks, i.e., four sides and four corner centers. Slip-stitch together. Steam and press all seams again.

Suggestions for making the Island Temple Scenic pillow in D.M.C. cotton follow.

B

C

A

Bind a piece of #14 canvas measuring 14″ by 17″. Bind a strip of #14 canvas measuring 50″ in length and 6″ in width. (Finished pillow will measure about 10″ x 13″ x 2″.) Use all 6 strands for working.

Two possible sets of colors follow:

I	II
Tone #1 822 off-white	3072 porcelain white
Tone #2 3013 light olive	3325 light blue
Tone #3 3012 medium olive	334 light medium blue
Tone #4 3011 olive	332 medium blue
Tone #5 935 green	312 dark medium blue
Tone #6 823 navy	311 navy blue

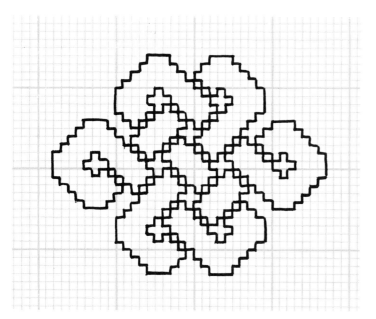

*Two small motifs which can be used alone
or in combination with others*

Bumblebee Pillow, Boxed

12" x 16" x 2½"

The face of the canvas measures 141 threads by 191 threads. The flaps are 31 stitches deep. Bind a piece of #12 canvas measuring 21" x 25". Then mark your outlines including those for the flaps. Mark the center threads and graph lines in the area on the surface of the pillow where you will work the bumblebee.

The following tones and colors are suggested for the bumblebee pillow:

1. Light   Off-White
2. Medium light   Putty
3. Medium   Gold
4. Medium dark   Olive Brown
5. Dark   Black

Photograph of actual pillow on page 60

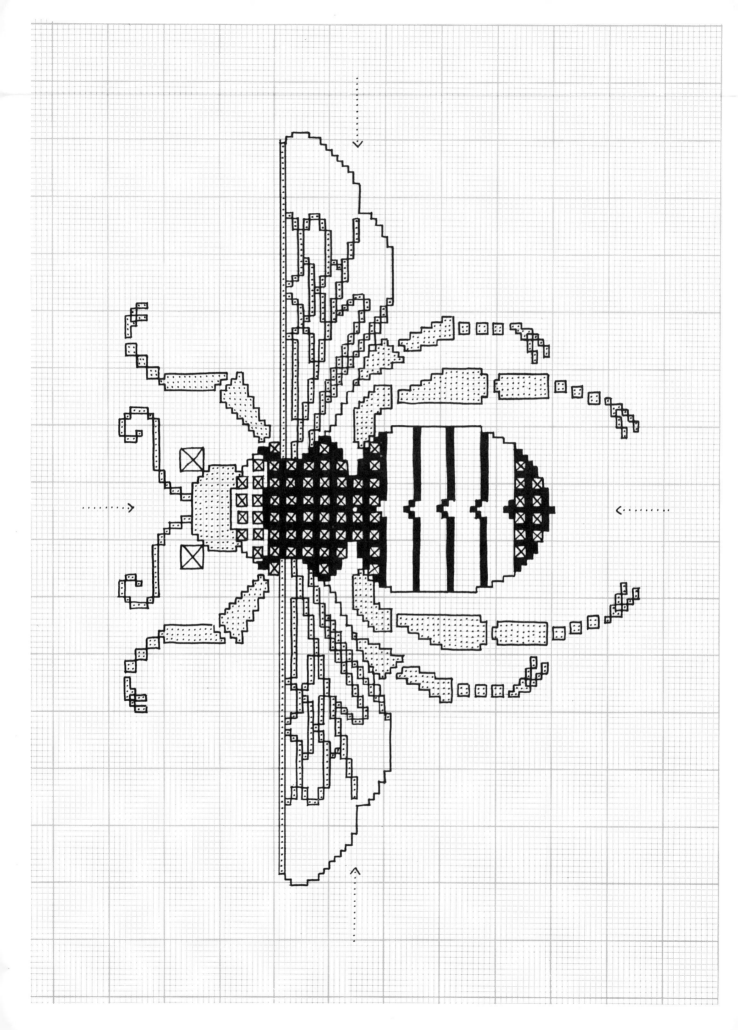

NOTE: There is a white dot in the middle of the bee's waist. It represents the intersection of the center threads of the canvas. Use it for reference when you begin work.

1. Using #4 tone work the dark parts of the bee's body. These are black on the graph. The small squares appearing in these two areas have, however, been left white in order that the symbol for the Smyrna cross stitch will be obvious. First work the Smyrna cross stitches, then fill in the rest of the dark areas, including the stripes. Then work the head and the antennae, or feelers.

2. Using #3 tone work Smyrna cross stitches behind bee's head. Then fill in background in this area. Work light areas between stripes on bee's body. Work double Leviathan stitches for eyes.

3. Using #2 tone work the veins in the wings.

4. Using #1 tone work the wings. I find it best to outline, then fill in.

5. Using #4 tone work the 6 legs.

6. Using #5 tone work key fret around edge of face of pillow.

7. Using #1 tone work background of key fret border.

8. Using #5 tone fill in background of face of pillow.

9. Using #1 tone work white band and broken X on each flap. NOTE: Work top and bottom flaps with stitches slanting in same direction as stitches on face of pillow. Work side flaps with stitches slanting at right angles to stitches on face of pillow.

10. Using #3 tone work "frog" pattern, which is the knot and bow design on the flaps.

11. Using #5 tone work background of flaps.

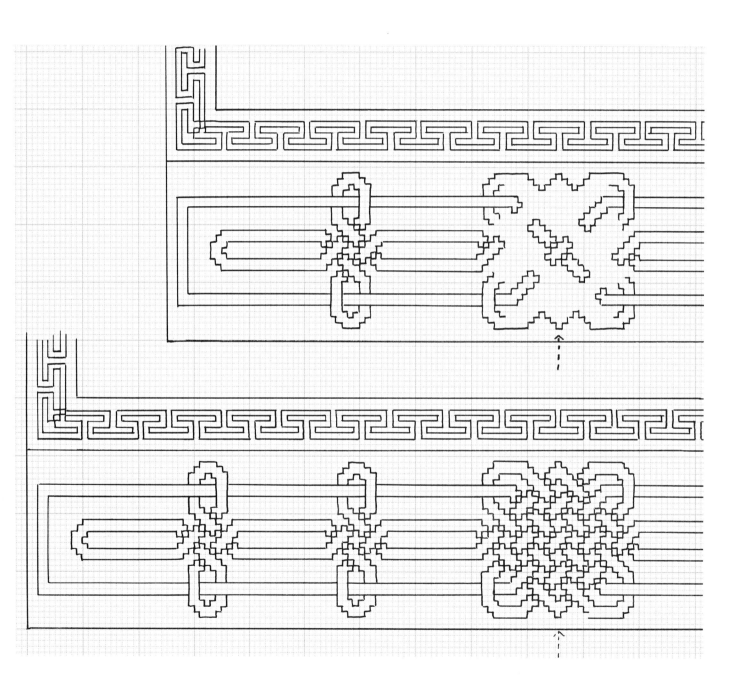

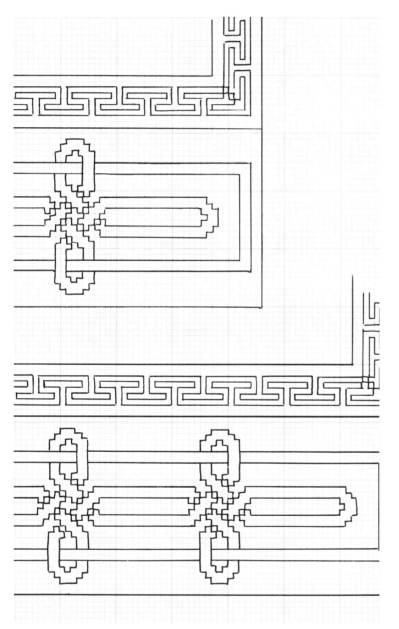

SIDE FLAPS

TOP AND BOTTOM FLAPS

NOTE: Below is a graphed diamond-shaped area for initials. Use it on the bottom flap in place of the center knot if you wish to sign your work.

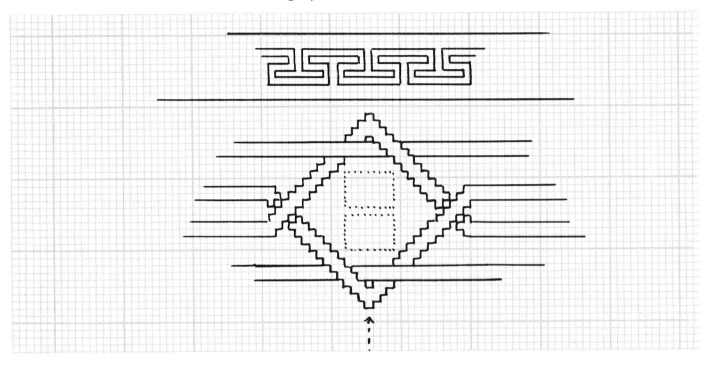

Butterfly Pillow, Boxed
12" x 16" x 2½"

The face of the canvas measures 141 threads by 191 threads. The flaps are 31 stitches deep. Bind a piece of #12 canvas measuring 21" x 25". Mark your outlines including those for the flaps. Mark center threads. Then mark the graph lines in the area on the surface of the pillow where you will work the butterfly.

The following 7 tones and colors are suggested for the butterfly pillow:

1. Light   Off-White
2. Medium light   Putty
3. Medium   Gold
4. Medium   Burnt-Orange
5. Medium dark   Olive Brown
6. Dark   Royal Navy
7. Dark   Black

NOTE: On the graph a white dot in the upper part of the diamond on the body of the butterfly represents the intersection of the center threads on the canvas. Use it for reference when you begin work.

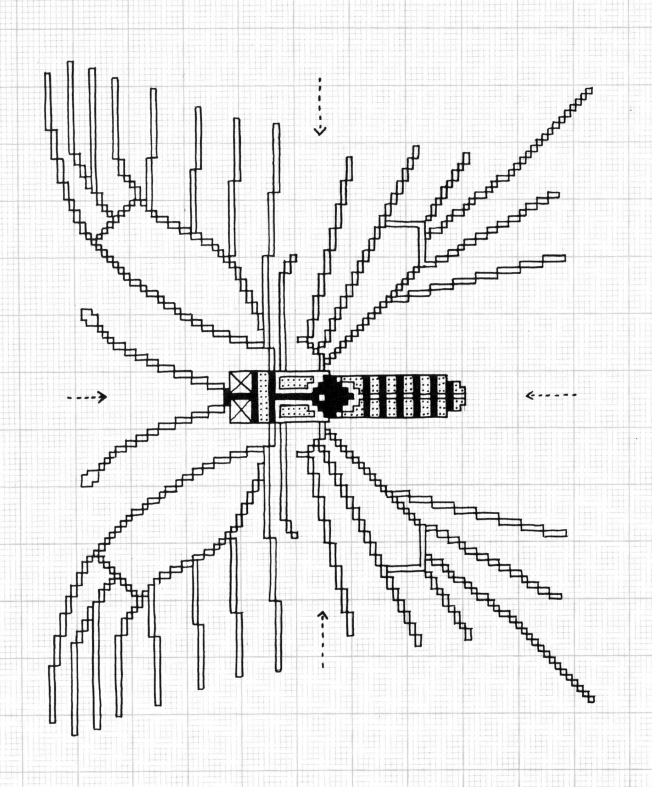

1. Using #6 tone work black lines and diamond in butterfly's body.

2. Using #3 tone work light lines in body.

3. Using #5 tone work dotted or shaded areas in body.

4. Using full strand of #4 tone work double Leviathan stitches for eyes.

5. Using #3 tone work antennae, or feelers.

6. Using #2 tone work veins in butterfly's wings.

   This graph shows only the body and veins of wings, to make starting the design easier. The full design is shown on the next two pages.

7. Using #3 tone work white areas in tips of upper wings. Then work areas at roots of wings as shown in illustration.

8. Using #5 tone work shaded or dotted areas in upper and lower wings.

9. Using #6 tone work black pattern at edges of lower wings.

10. Using #1 tone work the white areas of the wings.

11. Using #7 tone work key fret pattern of border. I work it in three steps: see illustration.

    a. Work stitches shown in black.
    b. Work stitches shown in white.
    c. Work row of dotted stitches.

12. Using #1 tone work background of key fret.

13. Using #7 tone fill in background of face of pillow.

14. Work flaps as indicated in directions for bumblebee (page 57).

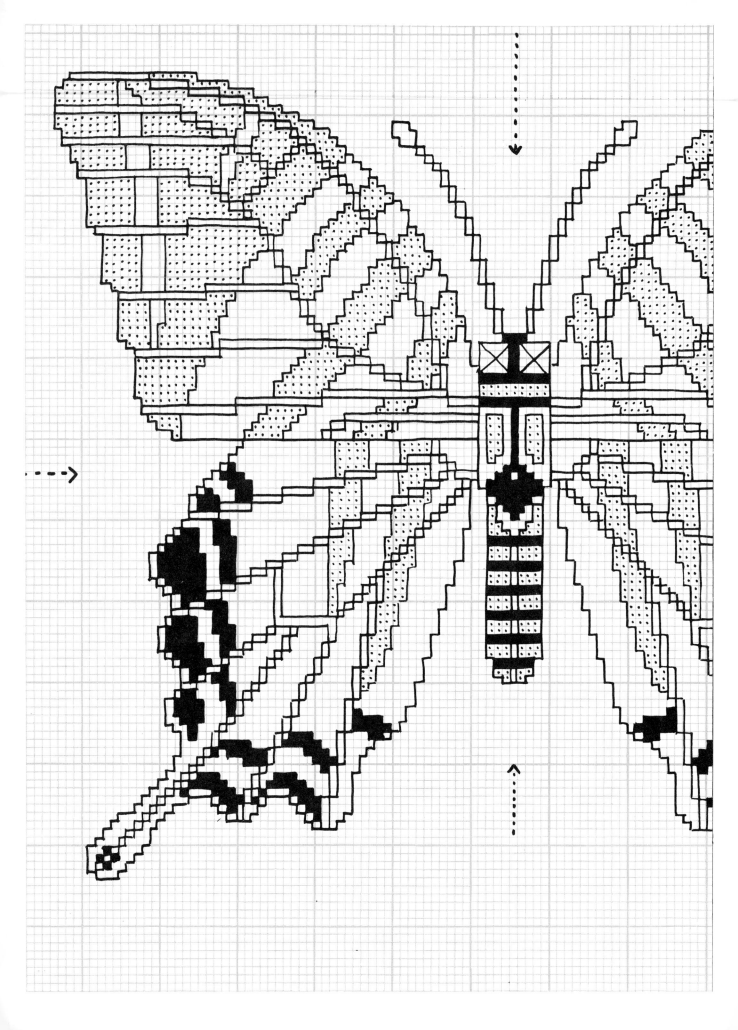

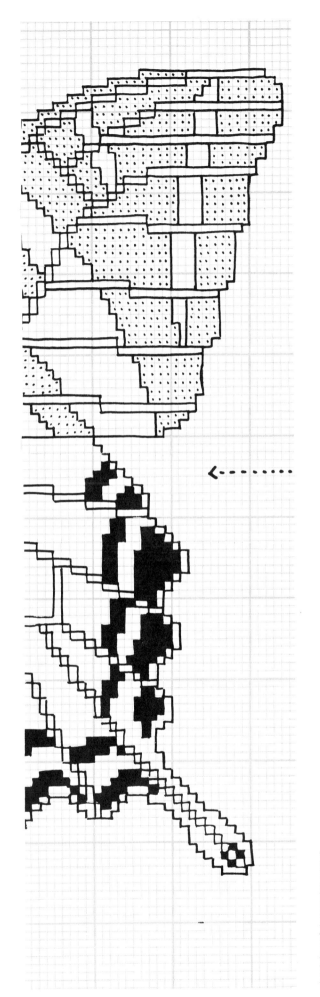

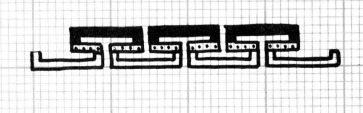

Circular Floral Pillow I, Boxed
11" diameter, 2½" boxing

Bind 2 pieces of #12 canvas, one 15" square for the face of the pillow, and one 40" x 6" for the boxing. Mark the center lines and the graph lines on the square piece. Do not try to mark the outline of the circle. You will do this by counting when you work the outer border in wool.

Count off and outline 385 threads for the length of the boxing, and 31 threads for the width if you plan to work the butterfly band, or 27 threads for the width if you plan to work the fluttering ribbon band.

An X at the top of the fretwork vase marks the center of the graph. It corresponds to the crossing of the two center threads on your canvas. Use this mark as a point of reference when you begin work.

Five tones and colors are suggested for the floral pillow:

1. Light   Off-White
2. Medium light   Pale Blue
3. Medium   Blue
4. Medium dark   Deep Blue
5. Dark   Navy

1. Using #3 tone work the fretwork vase, including the tassels and handle, i.e., that part of the vase marked in black on the graph.

2. Using #2 tone work the dotted or shaded portion of the vase, including the tassels.

3. Using #1 and #3 tone work flower in the square in the middle of the fat part of the vase, then fill in the background of the square with #2.

4. Using #3 tone work all the flower stems except the two marked in black on the graph. Work these either in #2 or #4 tone. Work the leaves in light and dark, #2 and #4.

5. Work the flowers. The two large ones at the top should be worked in the following manner: #4 where it is shown in black on the graph, #3 where it is shown dotted or shaded, #2 for the white petals, and #1 for the center, with #5 for the dots.

6. The downward-facing flowers at the ends of the 2 arched stems, black stems on the graph, should be done as follows: #4 tone for the black lines, #3 tone for the dotted or shaded portions, and #2 tone for the upper sides of the flowers.

Two alternate designs for the boxing band are shown on pages 70 and 71.

7. Work all the other flowers.

8. Using #1 tone work two dotted bands around the face of the pillow.

9. Using #2 tone work band between two shaded bands.

10. Using #5 tone work background of face of pillow.

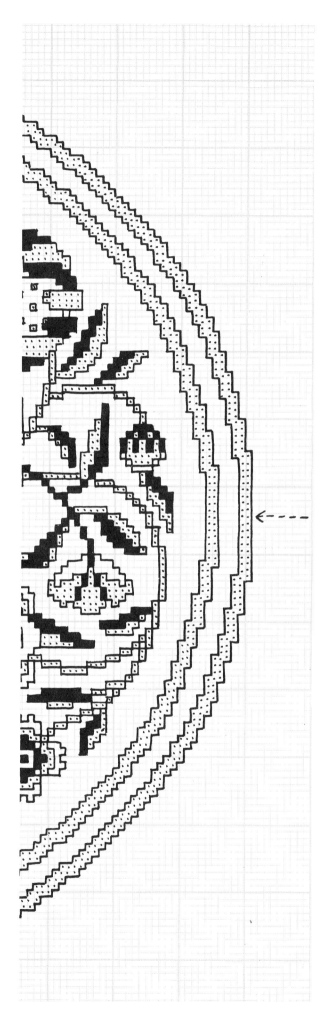

Circular Floral Pillow I,
Boxed

Butterfly Banding

1. Using #1 tone work outline of each panel.

2. Using #1 and #3 tones work body and antennae, or feelers of butterflies, #3 tone for shaded lines, #1 tone for white. #1 tone for eyes, black dots on graph.

3. Upper wings of butterfly shade from #1 in areas next to the body, through #2 and #3, to #4 at tips of wings, with two #1 dots. Under wings of butterfly shade from #2 tone next to the body out to #4 tone at tips of wings, with two #1 dots.

4. Using #5 tone fill in background inside panels.

5. Using #2 tone work background of boxing band.

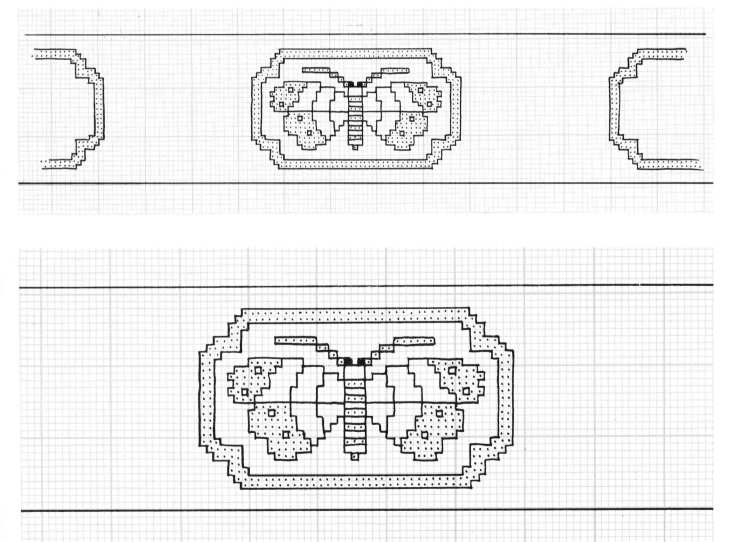

Fluttering Ribbon Banding

1. Using #5 tone for white part of ribbons and #1 tone for dotted or shaded areas on graph, work fluttering ribbon motifs.

2. Using #2 tone work background of boxing band.

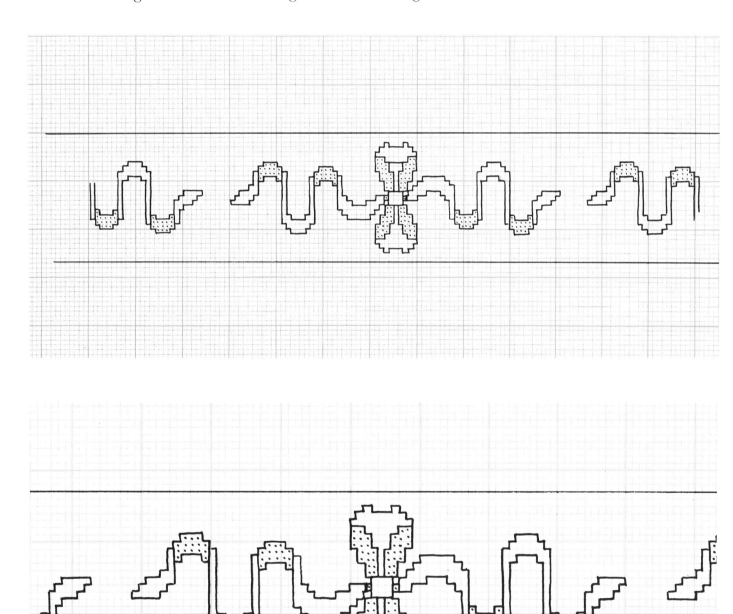

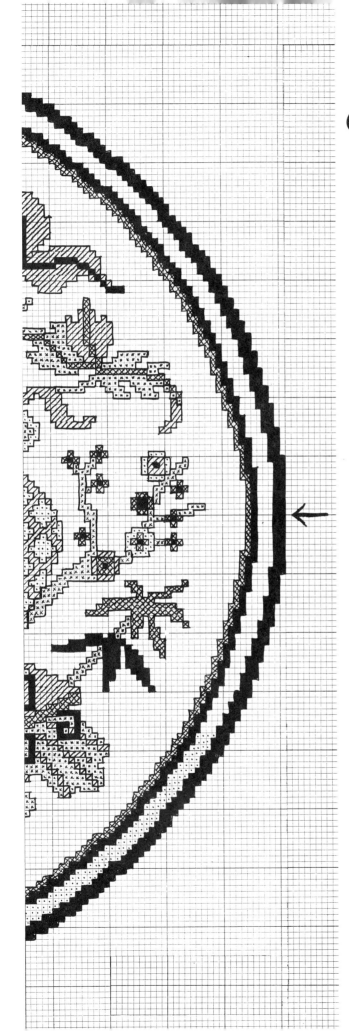

Circular Floral Pillow II

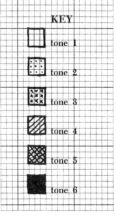

	KEY
	tone 1
	tone 2
	tone 3
	tone 4
	tone 5
	tone 6

Circular Floral Pillow II
13¾" diameter with 2½" boxing

The square within which the circle fits measures 162 by 162 threads. Bind a piece of #12 canvas measuring 18" x 18". Mark horizontal and vertical center lines. Mark the outlines of the square. Mark the graph lines within the work area.

There are six tones in the design. They are:

1. White
2. Light
3. Light medium
4. Medium
5. Medium dark
6. Dark

The original pillow was made with Persian wool. The key to the colors used follows:

1. 005 white
2. 396 pale blue
3. 386 light medium blue
4. 385 medium blue
5. 330 medium dark blue
6. 365 navy blue

This design was taken from an antique Chinese plate recently found in the ash pile of an early colonial military encampment on the eastern coast of Canada. The plate had evidently been discarded because badly broken. When found, however, it was pieced together and photographed for an art magazine. There I saw it and felt that it would lend itself well to needlepoint. Since the design was originally created for porcelain, I think it should be worked in traditional glaze colors, such as olive, deep to pale, or eggplant, from dark to faded amethyst, for example.

The graph has been drawn with tonal symbols in each square so no instructions are necessary for the placement of tones.

Boxing Band

For the boxing band bind a strip of canvas 55″ in length by 6″ in width. The working area measures 505 threads in length by 31 threads in width. Mark it off with graph lines in the areas where the panels will be worked. Each panel measures 45 threads from end to end and 25 threads from top to bottom. The panels are separated by areas measuring 56 threads in length. Place the panels on the strip as follows:

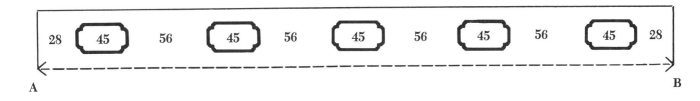

When you are ready to join the band to the face of the pillow you must first join the two ends together. Fold the panel in half with the inside out. Sew the two ends together by hand using #2 wool thread. For a neat seam, match the canvas threads of one end to the corresponding canvas threads of the other end. Press seam open. Pin the side of the band between A and B to the face of the pillow. I first mark three lines on the

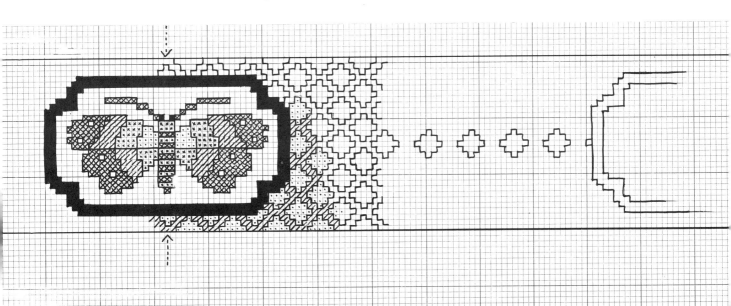

band: the center and halfway from center to one end. These three lines match the center top and the two side centers on the face of the pillow. The band seam, of course, goes to the bottom center. After pinning the band all the way around, sew the band to the face of the pillow by hand, using #2 wool thread. Do not catch in seam allowances of boxing band. Press around-the-pillow seam toward boxing.

For the back of the pillow cut a circle of silk and wool that matches the #2 tone. Make it 1½" larger in diameter than the face of the pillow. Use the sewing machine to baste, on the backing, the outline of a circle exactly matching the size of the face of the pillow. Put your custom-made pillow inside the needlework band (already joined to face of pillow cover). Turn in raw edge of banding. Pin banding to backing along basting line. Slip-stitch. Give a final touch up by pressing the pillow once with a damp cloth and a steam iron.

If you plan to make the Circular Floral pillow in D.M.C cotton floss, follow the preceding directions, but use #14 canvas for a pillow which, when finished, will measure 11½" in diameter with a boxing slightly deeper than 2".

Suggested colors are:

1. 3072, or use blanc neige
2. 827 light blue
3. 813 medium light blue
4. 826 medium blue
5. 825 medium dark blue
6. 824 dark blue

Suggestions for French silk colors are:

	BLUES	GREENS	LAVENDERS
1.	73 blanc	73 blanc	73 blanc
2.	1711	1841	4631
3.	1712	1842	4632
4.	1713	1843	4634
5.	1714	1844	4645
6.	1716	1845	4646

Dove at a Branch of Peach Blossoms
OCTAGON 17" in diameter

After a painting by Emperor Hui Tsung, Sung Dynasty.

The square within which the octagonal pillow fits measures 226 threads by 226 threads. Bind a piece of #14 canvas measuring 21" x 21". Mark horizontal and vertical center lines. Outline square, then draw graph lines in work area. (For outer frame see diagram on page 80 and use double straight cross stitch.)

Fourteen colors of D.M.C. cotton were used in the original pillow. The key to their numbers and their placement in the design follows:

926 medium teal blue
> Use for top of head, dotted on graph; and upper part of beak, shaded on graph.

Blanc neige, white
> Use for outline of eye; upper root of beak; buds and flowers; step 5 of breast, i.e., lower forward part of bird's body; and for two lower horizontal bands in wings.

645 dark gray
> Use for dark line in beak; and for feet.

301 bittersweet
> Use for shaded area in eye (iris is 3371 brown), and for initials. (Use your own.)

3052 gray-green
> Use for 1st step of breast shading, i.e., large area under head; and for stems of flowers, dotted on graph.

3053 gray-green
> Use for 2nd step of breast shading, i.e., top step of three shallow steps left white on graph; and for dotted lines in lower body.

3013 soft green-gold
> Use for 3rd step of breast shading; and for BACKGROUND.

3072 pale gray-green

Use for 4th step of breast shading. (Fifth step under blanc neige.)

3011 olive

Use for shaded area at back of neck; and with 3021 brown for double cross stitch on bird's back, i.e., large unshaded areas. Outline first with brown, then work diagonal cross stitches in olive. Finally, fill in empty holes with upright cross stitches in brown. Use 3011 olive for shaded area between back and wing; for dotted areas in wings; and for three dotted bands in upper part of tail.

3021 brown

Use with 3011 olive in double cross stitch on back of bird; and for x'd areas in upper and lower tail.

3371 dark brown

Use for black areas in wing and tail; and for iris in eye.

640 fawn brown

Use for branches of trees.

3051 sage green

Use for outline of central octagon; outlines of eight border panels; and for shaded band in outer border, near edge of pillow.

Work the brick stitch within the inner octagon, i.e., around the bird and branches (all worked in basket-weave). I use the brick stitch turned over on its side. Work the basket-weave around and between panels, and for outer border.

For this pillow I used the same textured stitch for all eight border panels. My choice was the double straight cross stitch. Diagram for outer border is shown on pages 80 and 82.

The pillow requires a 2″ fabric boxing. Match it to 3051 sage green. Cut a strip 60″ in length and 3½″ in width. For complete instructions on applying boxing bands and backing, turn to page 75.

A Magpie on a Flowering Branch
OCTAGON 17" in diameter

Detail from a painting in the style
of the Sung Dynasty.
THE METROPOLITAN MUSEUM OF ART.

The square within which the octagonal pillow fits measures 226 threads by 226 threads. Bind a piece of #14 canvas measuring 21" x 21". Mark horizontal and vertical center lines. Outline square, then draw graph lines in work area. (Work outer frame in alternating 4-thread squares of square eyelet and basket-weave.)

Twenty tones and colors of French silk were used in the original pillow. The key to their numbers and their placement in the design follows:

2636 red for beak, claws, and initials (use your own initials)
3414 medium gray in head and lower wings
3415 medium dark gray in head and lower wings
3416 dark gray in head and lower wings
2232 light gold for breast and tail
2234 medium gold for breast and tail
2235 dark gold for breast
3433 light mauve gray in upper wing
3434 medium mauve gray in upper wing
3435 dark mauve gray in upper wing
3845 dark gray spots in tail
3833 brown for branches
3834 darker brown for outlining branches
3723 light green for leaves
3724 medium green for leaves
3725 dark green for leaves
Blanc white for flowers in foreground. Work in double straight
cross stitch.

3711 off-white in tail and white flowers in background. Work
latter in double straight cross stitch.
3712 taupe background color
3713 darker taupe for outlining border panels and pillow

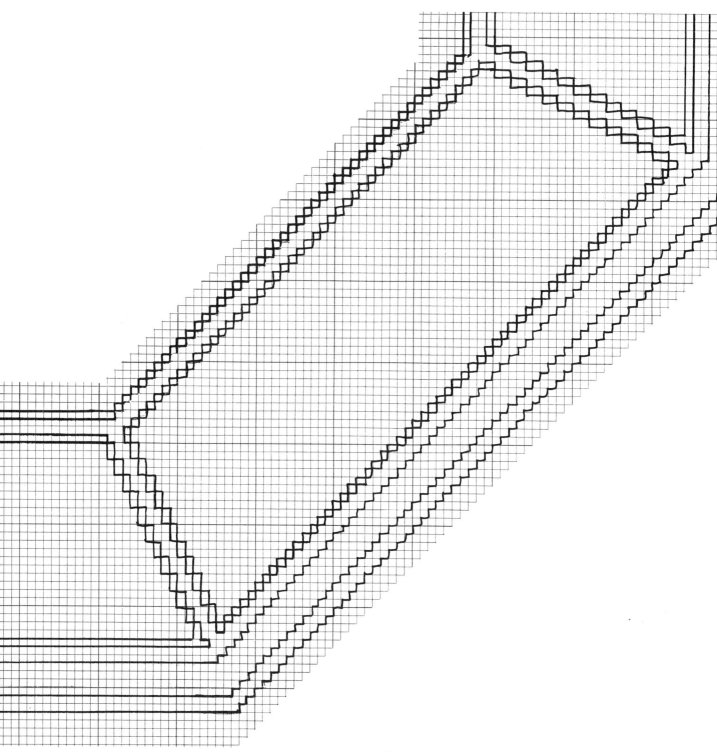

Geometric Pillow
19" x 19" (approximately)

The face of the Geometric pillow measures 227 threads by 227 threads. Bind a piece of #12 canvas measuring 24" x 24". Mark the center threads, outline the work area, and mark graph lines in the field.

Three tones and colors of Paternayan Persian wool were used in the sample pillow. The key follows:

    010 white for light
    440 yellow for medium
    330 blue for dark

When working this pillow I drew directly on the canvas the outlines for the border bands, the eight patterned areas, and the eight lozenges containing the eternal knots. The only areas where the graph lines could be helpful are: the center field, and within each of the eight lozenges where you will work the eternal knots. The eight patterned areas need only horizontal and vertical center lines.

HELPFUL HINTS: While working the pattern in the field, first work the outlines of the swastika design. It is a repeat that you can soon learn. Fill it in later. When working the eternal knots, I work the "holes" first, using the background color, then work the knots around the holes.

NOTE: In the sample pillow, for the narrow, two-row outline bands I used a straight stitch over the two canvas threads (three strands of wool to cover) and pivoted at each corner.

For the outer border I used the Irish stitch, mitering each corner (again using three strands of wool to cover). These stitches work up quickly and are attractive, but you may, if you prefer, work the entire pillow in the basket-weave.

This design is very flexible. You may change the tonal values and colors in this pillow as long as you follow the basic scheme used in the sample, i.e., use light where I have used dark, or light where I have used medium, or dark where I have used medium. If you like one patterned area particularly, use it for all the patterned areas in the border.

This design can even be worked on a #8 penelope canvas to make a small rug. When working with this mesh, use three strands of wool to cover. If you want a long rug rather than a square one, you can plan your own adaptation by drawing it on graph paper.